DESIGNED TO LAST

RENOVATE YOUR FINANCIAL HOUSE AND RETIRE WITH CONFIDENCE.

JUSTIN M. BIANCE, CEP®

JUSTIN M. BIANCE/DESIGNED TO LAST—1ST EDITION

735 5th Avenue West
Hendersonville, NC 28739
https://jbiance.com/
ISBN 9798595435079

INVESTMENT ADVISOR DISCLOSURE

Justin Biance is registered as an investment advisor representative and is a licensed insurance agent in the states of Florida and North Carolina. J. Biance Financial is an independent financial services firm that helps individuals create retirement strategies using a variety of investment and insurance products to custom suit their needs and objectives. Investment advisory services are offered only by dually registered individuals through AE Wealth Management, LLC (AEWM). AEWM and J. Biance Financial are not affiliated companies. The firm is not affiliated with the Social Security Administration, Medicare, or any other governmental agency.

The contents of this book are provided for informational purposes only and are not intended to serve as the basis for any financial decisions. Any tax, legal, or estate planning information is general in nature. It should not be construed as legal or tax advice. Always consult an attorney or tax professional regarding the applicability of this information to your unique situation.

Information presented is believed to be factual and up to date, but we do not guarantee its accuracy and it should not be regarded as a complete analysis of the subjects discussed. All expressions of opinion are those of the author as of the date of publication and are subject to change. Content should not be construed as personalized investment advice, nor should it be interpreted as an offer to buy or sell any securities mentioned. A financial advisor should be consulted before implementing any of the strategies presented.

Investing involves risk, including the potential loss of principal. No investment strategy can guarantee a profit or protect against loss in periods of declining values. Any references to protection benefits or guaranteed/lifetime income streams refer only to fixed insurance products, not securities or investment products. Insurance and annuity product guarantees are backed by the issuing insurance company's financial strength and claims-paying ability.

CONTENTS

———

FOR THE CLIENTS OF
J. BIANCE FINANCIAL
Thank you for being part of our family;
it is an honor to serve you.

FOREWORD

———

Like most younger brothers, I lived in Justin's shadow a bit growing up. We are nineteen months apart, and during our childhood, we were both curious and adventurous. We enjoyed competing, no matter the game. Our spontaneous wrestling matches that happened all over the house caused our grandparents to regularly raise their voices: "Take it outside, you're going to break something!" They loved helping raise us— Justin, our sister Wendi and myself—but I think "the boys" may have contributed to their need for blood pressure medicine.

Based on the frequency with which my brother and I spent competing, one might think we were always at odds with one another. And in fairness, to some degree, we were. Golf, home run derby, pushup contests, ping pong, you name it, the rivalry existed. He is a Florida State Seminole and I am a Florida Gator. However, beyond team rivalries and competitive games, we were inseparable. When we were young, I did not realize all the things he was teaching me. The things I learned from Justin were many times caught, not necessarily taught. It is amazing what you can pick up from a person, simply by watching their actions. I am just glad I picked my favorite college team at a very young age—before he could accidentally steer me down the wrong path.

I have been fortunate to benefit from many of Justin's life experiences, especially when it comes to do-it-yourself (DIY) projects. Justin and Angela have owned several houses, both old and new; you will enjoy reading about a few of those houses in this book. The projects have varied widely, and the lessons learned during these adventures have been, well, memorable.

One of my favorite projects was back in 2018 when he and Angela had 20 members of our family at their house for Thanksgiving. Earlier in the week, Justin had to dig a 60-foot ditch to lay a new septic pipe. He thought he had fixed the only problem in the guest bathroom just in time for the extended families' arrivals. I was sitting in the living room when Monroe, Justin's oldest son, ran in and said there was water leaking into the garage below the bathroom. We peeled back drywall in both the bathroom and the garage and finally found the nail-punctured copper pipe in the wall.

We turned off the main water line and headed to the hardware store for supplies. Without running water, most of the Thanksgiving dinner preparations had to cease—except a little baking. Upon arriving back home from our second trip to the hardware store, we walked into the house and encountered what some may describe as mayhem.

While we were gone, the oven had caught fire. Flour was spread everywhere (used to put out the fire), and no water to clean it up. We got to work immediately and fixed the leak. After we had running water again, we helped clean up the kitchen. With a new pipe in the bathroom and running water to clean up the kitchen, we were happy that things had improved. We decided to go back down in the garage, where the saga began, to make sure the waterfall from the bathroom above had stopped. The good news was the leak was fixed. The bad news was the neighbor's dog was enjoying his Thanksgiving meal. Unbeknownst to anyone upstairs, a local farm had delivered the 30-pound turkey that was to be part of our meal and had left it downstairs near the garage. I think it is safe to say that dog never had such a tasty Thanksgiving.

I would imagine many of you have performed home repair projects. They can be a lot of fun, but they can also be extremely challenging. I find that as people get older, they tend to hire someone to help with projects like fixing a leak in the bathroom. Retirement is about relaxing, and DIY projects can sometimes make it hard to relax! I also find that retirees often feel they are juggling multiple concerns at once. Whether repairing a financial mistake or putting out a financial fire, tackling investment, income, healthcare, taxes, and legacy questions can make for a stressful instead of a stress-free retirement. If you are reading this book, I would imagine you would like to focus on those things that matter most to you: your children, your grandkids, your hobbies, and your travel goals. Whether it is a home DIY project or a financial DIY project, both can distract you from those more important things in life.

Our holistic wealth managers, or as we like to call them, our "retirement engineers," are solely focused on creating a blueprint for your financial future. Through our experience guiding hundreds of pre-retirees and retirees through our Retirement Design System®, we have helped people like you answer the biggest and most important questions about retirement. "Will I outlive my money?" "Can I afford long-term care?" "How will taxes affect my retirement?" Reading this book will help you answer these questions and many more.

Justin will guide you through our clear and straightforward process, which will help you make sense of this complex season called retirement. In addition to your money, you also need to feel free to focus on your two most valuable assets: your family and your time. Through family and client stories, Justin will help you learn new ways to protect and enrich both.

The renovation of your financial house should begin with this book. I am excited for you and your family. These pages contain an immense amount of insight to help you gain confidence about your retirement. Let the project of designing your ideal retirement begin!

- JASON C. BIANCE, CFP®
CO-FOUNDER, J. BIANCE FINANCIAL

INTRODUCTION

I gained perspective on retirement for the first time when I was seven years old. After my parents divorced, my mom's parents, Grandma and Grandpa Carta, moved in. My grandparents added a lot to our family. In some ways, they filled the void in our home that existed after the divorce. They also gave me a first-hand encounter of what retirement looks like.

My grandparents' weekly routine looked something like: A) schedule doctors' appointments, B) go to doctors' appointments, C) come home and schedule next week's doctors' appointments. Repeat. With doctors came bills, and their cloud of money worries was obvious, even at my young age.

Grandpa's morning routine included using his magnifying glass to follow his stocks in the newspaper. His blood pressure would rise and fall with the stock market. Grandma would walk laps around our house, helping Mom with the laundry. Even when she started using a walker, Grandma would wedge the laundry basket between the walker and slide it across the tile floor. She didn't mind that walking. The walk that worried her was the walk to the mailbox and the fear that her Social Security check wouldn't arrive. I didn't realize it then but living with retirees showed the unique worries that come during that stage of life. Those worries were obviously different from mine as a boy, but they were also clearly different from the concerns of my parents, who were still working.

The perspective Grandma and Grandpa gave me is unfortunately hard to find in financial services. This industry wasn't designed for the pre-retiree and retiree. Most industry experts are absorbed with market capitalization, bond yields, and other indictators that do not really help you answer the question, "Will I outlive my money?"

THE HOUSE

Many pre-retirees go through a bit of an emotional rollercoaster before they retire. While there is a lot of excitement about being free from work, a new reality sets in: permanent unemployment. Then the questions rush in: How will I afford long-term care? Will my assets withstand a severe market correction? How much will I pay in taxes?

The concern surrounding retirement is instinctual. If any of these questions have come to mind, either while preparing for retirement or during retirement, they are completely natural, and a testament that you are reading the right book! Saving for retirement is like building a "financial house." The exterior shell (roof, walls, and foundation) is what I refer to as investment planning. The roof represents risky investments, the walls represent moderate investments, and the foundation represents guaranteed vehicles. Your financial house also has interior rooms, which represent income planning, healthcare planning, tax planning, and legacy planning. We will cover each of these rooms in the following chapters.

This book is going to reveal ways to help you renovate your financial house. If you have concerns or questions about any of the five areas of retirement—investment, income, healthcare, taxes, or legacy planning—don't ignore them. They need to be addressed. At the conclusion of each chapter, there is a page provided for you to capture your goals and concerns related to the area of planning covered in that chapter. At the end of the book, you will find a Retirement Renovation Questionnaire. These questions will help you do a little "walkthrough" of your financial house. When you retire or approach retirement, it is time to get your questions answered and to put a plan in place. Eliminate doubt. Make sure your financial house is *designed to last*.

THE SEASON

When an investor transitions from the accumulation phase (focus is acquiring assets) to the distribution phase (focus is living on those assets), the financial landscape can get more complicated. You blinked and, all of a sudden, thirty or forty years have gone by. You were busy working and saving and that was the only planning you did—work and save. Many Americans drift into retirement with a financial house that may not be strong enough to withstand an economic storm. To put it simply, renovations are needed.

Imagine you hired a contractor to build your dream home, and he started by building your roof, first! Believe it or not, your financial house was likely constructed this way. The typical progression of investing is not necessarily a prudent way to build a house. The financial house that working professionals build typically starts with a roof—*investments with more risk*. It could eventually include walls—*investments with moderate risk*. But early on, investors aren't worried about a foundation—*principal protected investments*. When you are young you take more risk, and you invest in a roof. It's okay to start with the roof when you are young because you won't live in this financial house (retire) for a long time. Once you get closer to retirement, however, you have to take a different approach.

As you get older, things change. The types of activities you enjoy change. The types of doctors you see change. Perhaps even how much you sleep or what you can eat, changes. When it comes to the retirement season of life, things change. A different season in life requires a different approach to your financial house.

THE GUIDE

Grandma and Grandpa Carta desired to live retirement richly. In some ways, having three grandkids in their home helped them achieve that, but they didn't have a substantial financial house. Their investments were all roof. No one ever helped them plan and design the interior rooms (income, healthcare, taxes, and legacy). Their financial house was incomplete. If you are retired or approaching retirement, you don't only need your money invested for you. You can easily do that yourself. It would help if you had a chief financial officer. A CFO would be someone who manages things for you so you can enjoy your retirement. The CFO would help answer your questions and help you not only survive retirement but, more importantly, thrive in retirement.

If you don't have a family CFO, you might end up with the job. You could become burdened with researching investment options, coordinating tax strategies with your CPA, making sure all your legal documents and beneficiaries are up to date—this list goes on and on. Or you can hire a guide. Your financial advisor is in a unique position to coordinate and help ensure that your entire financial landscape is in good order. Some in the financial services industry want you to believe that if an advisor provides investment advice and helps you invest your money, he has done his job. Don't buy it. Expect more. Your financial advisor should manage every part of your financial house: investment, income, healthcare, taxes, and legacy planning strategies—and do so without you asking! After visiting all the rooms of your financial house, I will describe what I believe you should look for in a financial advisor.

A holistic financial advisor or family CFO transforms money into a means to accomplish your goals instead of distracting you from them. In the final chapter, *The Front Porch*, I will share a few ways to help you find your "why" in retirement and achieve your goals. A robust financial house is vital. Without it, you will probably be worried about the next storm. Have you already retired and are now wondering if market risk, rising tax rates, large healthcare expenses, or some other unknown might make your goals unachievable? These are the questions, the distractions, that surrounded my grandparents' retirement. Their financial house needed renovation, but they didn't have a guide or a system to help them with the project. This book will provide you with details about both.

THE SYSTEM

Most retirees I meet desire more confidence about their retirement. However, confidence cannot be manufactured, and acting confident when you should be worried is not always harmless optimism—it might become a disaster. I believe that true financial confidence comes from true financial security. The confidence that comes with a rising stock market is fleeting and, as I am sure you have experienced, the weather on Wall Street can change very quickly. If you have a strong financial house, one prepared and renovated for retirement, you don't have to worry as much about an economic storm. You can focus on the best things in life like family, leisure, and loving service in gratitude for all you've received.

My brother, Jason, and I founded J. Biance Financial to help pre-retirees and retirees address the areas we witnessed our grandparents struggle with while growing up. Our team at J. Biance Financial helps Americans retire with the confidence to enjoy this time of their lives. Over the years, we have worked with hundreds of families. Every day, our advisors use our proprietary planning process, the Retirement Design System®, to help pre-retirees and retirees plan for the challenges that come with retirement. The following pages lay out the essential elements of that system so that you will have a time-tested process to renovate your financial house. We will walk through the parts of your financial house—investment, income, healthcare, taxes, and legacy planning strategies—and you will learn what a holistic retirement plan looks like. With this new perspective, you will have the tools to create a retirement plan that is *designed to last.*

*Before you read about each part of your financial house,
think about why you decided to read this book.*

What about your current financial situation would
you like to improve?

_____

_____

_____

_____

_____

_____

_____

_____

_____

_____

_____

_____

_____

CHAPTER 1

INVESTMENT PLANNING

THE EXTERIOR OF YOUR FINANCIAL HOUSE

My heart was racing as I sat in a cold chapel in Tallahassee, Florida, and prayed with my college sweetheart, Angela Hartley. I'm not sure if it really was cold or not; I may have just been shaking from nerves. It was hard to pray because I was about to ask Angela to marry me.

The proposal went beautifully. I knelt and asked Angela to be my bride, and she said yes. Well, she didn't say yes right away. As I started to go down on one knee, she asked in a shocked voice, "What are you doing?" But in the end, she said yes. That night started a wonderful year-long engagement. After we told family and friends that we would be married the following summer, it was time to start thinking about what that first year of marriage would look like: where and how we would begin our family. At some point, Angela's Aunt Mary recommended that we look at a little second-story apartment that was part of her grandmother's house in downtown Jacksonville, Florida.

The house Grandmother Hartley lived in was built in 1901. She lived downstairs, and the upstairs was a separate apartment. The house was next to the florist shop Grandmother Hartley owned. Grandmother's late husband, E.B., had opened Hartley the Florist in 1947, just before they were married. As a matter of fact, E.B. provided the flowers for their wedding—one of his first orders. The Hartleys raised their children in this old home, and fifty-six years later, Grandmother Hartley still lived downstairs. We were happy to find an affordable place with deep connections to Angela's family, but it came with challenges. Before we moved in, Grandmother Hartley had a string of bad tenants. They took advantage of her and almost destroyed the flat. The home had been renovated multiple times, but it was again in need of significant repairs and updating.

When we entered the apartment, it looked like it had been abandoned for decades. Grandmother didn't give us the tour because she was so upset about the apartment's condition and couldn't bear the sight. We found bird nests and trash everywhere and almost nothing worked. It needed a complete renovation from floor to ceiling. After we came downstairs, I looked at Angela, and she looked at me. I turned to Aunt Mary, who had given us the tour, and said, "I think this is perfect." Angela about fell over. She could not believe that I was even considering we could live there after we married. But after several hours of talking it through, I convinced Angela that I could renovate it on weekends throughout our year-long engagement. I promised it would be ready when we returned from our honeymoon.

I put together a detailed budget and a project list of everything I wanted to do. I presented it to Grandmother Hartley, and she said, "Justin, if you do all of that, I will pay for materials, and you can live there rent-free for your first year of marriage." I was thrilled. I spent every available weekend in Jacksonville working on that apartment. I even convinced four friends to spend their spring break with me renovating. We slept on the floor, ate a lot of pizza, and got a lot accomplished. Of course, it didn't all go smoothly, but the night before our wedding, I put the finishing touches of paint on the stairwell walls. As promised, we returned from our honeymoon and moved in.

TIME TO RENOVATE
Even as a young man, I knew Grandmother Hartley's home wasn't suitable for my new bride and our future

family. Our new home needed serious attention before we could enjoy it with any level of confidence. Different times in life require a home renovation. You get married and buy a fixer-upper, time to renovate. You and your spouse have your third child and need to add on, well, it's time to renovate. Your elderly parents can't live independently and need a wheelchair accessible bathroom, well, it's time to renovate. Numerous similarities exist between renovating a house and renovating for retirement. You are gainfully employed, but there isn't room in your budget for retirement saving, time to renovate. You are about to retire and live on your savings, well, it's time to renovate. Like any house renovation, tackling a financial fixer-upper can be exciting and challenging, but it will give you more confidence about retirement after the project is complete.

If we are going to make sure your financial house will hold up in a storm, we must design it well. As you can see from the illustration below, the exterior of your financial house has three main sections: the roof, the walls, and the foundation. The roof typically comprises the more aggressive investments (e.g., stocks, private equity). When a financial storm comes, these are usually the first to be affected. The walls comprise less volatile investments (e.g., corporate debt, fixed income), but damage to the roof can work its way down to the walls. And finally, there is the foundation (e.g., insurance products, bank products). No matter how bad the storm is, the foundation isn't going anywhere if properly constructed. How do you know if your financial house is properly constructed? You need a building code to follow, an objective standard to measure against, so you know your calculations are correct.

ROOF
- Stocks & Private Equity
- Small, Mid & Large Cap Funds
- Sector ETFs

WALLS
- Real Estate
- Hard Assets
- Bonds/Fixed Income

FOUNDATION
- Cash & CDs
- Insurance Products
- Treasury Inflation
  Protected Securities (TIPS)

Bank products are FDIC-insured up to applicable limits, whereas insurance products are guaranteed by the financial strength and claims-paying ability of the issuing company.

Investments are subject to risk, including possible loss of principal.

YOUR FINANCIAL BUILDING CODE

During that first renovation of Grandmother Hartley's house, I made a few calculations that set me back. The worst was measuring the carpet for our bedroom six inches too short. It's not fun to roll out a new carpet and learn that no matter how much you stretch it, it's not going to make it to the wall! To design a financial house properly, we are going to do a lot of measuring. Precision is essential—we can't just get close. As the old adage goes, "Close only counts in horseshoes and hand grenades." When you start building your financial house, you must pay close attention to your investments' risk. You must be precise, and to be precise, it is essential to measure your risk with a number, not a word. Strangely, in financial services, a lot of advisors describe your risk tolerance with a word and not a number.

Have you ever walked into a broker's office, and one of the first things you do is take a risk tolerance questionnaire? These tests ask you basic questions and then classify you into one of five primary levels based on your answers. Those levels (Morningstar Risk Classifications[1]) are conservative, moderately conservative, moderate, moderately aggressive, and aggressive. It is important to know your risk tolerance, but do you think one of these five classifications really says anything about how much money you can stand to lose?

---

[1]James Chen. Investopedia. March 26, 2020. "Morningstar Risk Rating" https://www.investopedia.com/terms/m/morningstarriskrating.asp.

Let's say there were a hundred people in a room, all classified as having a moderate risk tolerance, and their portfolios were all invested based on a moderate rating. Do you think they would all react *in precisely the same way* if they experienced a stock market correction? Do you think if they were each asked to define a devastating loss, they would answer in the same way? The five classifications don't say enough about your risk tolerance. It's simply not specific enough.

Investor behavior has been studied for decades. Recent research suggests people make very different decisions when the element of risk is part of the equation.[2] In our practice, we use a quantitative tool built on a Nobel Prize-winning behavioral study to determine our clients' risk tolerance. This tool, however, doesn't provide any of the five risk ratings above. It assigns a risk number. That makes sense, doesn't it? When we're talking finances, we're talking about numbers. There's plenty in life that we can't put a number or value on, but we need to know the number for many things. Do you drive too fast? Check your speedometer (number). Is your cholesterol too high? Check your LDLs and HDLs (numbers). Did your grandson do well on the SAT? Check his exam score (number). Risk tolerance should probably inform your investment decisions in the accumulation phase, but we definitely need to see where we stand once we get to the distribution phase. We need a

---

[2]Daniel Kahneman and Amos Tversky, "Prospect Theory: An Analysis Of Decision Under Risk,", Econometrica (pre-1986); 47, no. 2 March 1979:263-292.

number. Whether your advisor uses a risk number or a similar tool to identify your unique risk tolerance, don't settle for the five categories above (conservative, moderate, etc.) It's more important now than ever before.

CONSTRUCTION BEGINS

Once we know your risk number, we can begin renovating the financial house so that it is ready for you to move in for retirement. Even if the initial analysis reveals that the roof leaks or the walls have weaknesses, or the foundation is cracked, don't panic. Instead, we can look at the situation objectively, make the necessary financial renovations, and then you can hopefully move in with lasting confidence.

Let's consider Susan Smith (a hypothetical client). After taking our risk assessment, we discover that Susan has a personal risk number of 43. Knowing Susan's risk number is 43 helps us determine into which areas of her estate that we will invest: roof, walls, and foundation.

Reviewing the diagram below, you can see how we might get to a portfolio close to a risk profile of 43 (note: we typically design within a four-point range). In the roof, we have various institutional mutual funds, stocks, and ETFs. Each holding in the roof has a specific risk number. Once we have selected all of the roof holdings for Susan's portfolio, we can get an average number for the roof. The combination of her roof holdings is a risk number of 78. Now you might think,

"Wow, that is pretty aggressive for a client who is only a 43." But remember, this is only the roof portion of Susan's total portfolio, and it accounts for about 30 percent of her total assets. The goal of the roof is growth, or as they say in baseball, to "swing for the fences." If the market goes up 10, 20, or 30 percent, we want to capture that gain with this portion of Susan's portfolio.

Moving on to the walls portion of Susan's portfolio, we might invest this money in various debt instruments such as corporate bonds. The goal of the walls is to generate income. Is there risk in the walls? Yes, but not as much as the roof. When the next financial hurricane comes, Susan's walls may experience some damage, but the roof will absorb the heaviest blow. After we select the holdings for Susan's walls—each has a specific risk number—the average risk number of the walls portion of her portfolio is 40, and we will allocate 30 percent of the portfolio to the walls.

Now that we have chosen her roof and walls' investments, it is time to address the foundation. The foundation of the portfolio is the most challenging portion of the financial house. Of the three sections, the foundation requires the greatest attention to detail and an extra measure of due diligence, because like a house, if the foundation is wrong, it can jeopardize the entire structure. Some of these investments are found in the securities world, such as Treasury Inflation Protected Securities (or TIPS for short). However, to allocate funds to some of these foundation products, we need to leave the securities world and look for solutions in the banking or insurance world. In Susan's case, we attribute 40 percent of her money to the foundation, which has a risk number of 1. As you can see, with the proper percentage of funds allocated to her roof, walls, and foundation, her portfolio, or the "exterior" of her financial house merits a risk number of 42. Since Susan is a 43, and we are within four points of her number, we can be confident that her portfolio is properly aligned with her risk tolerance.

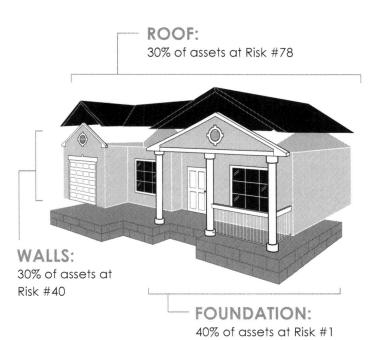

ROOF:
30% of assets at Risk #78

WALLS:
30% of assets at
Risk #40

FOUNDATION:
40% of assets at Risk #1

TOTAL PORTFOLIO: RISK #42

Example shown for illustrative purposes only. Your actual portfolio will vary by your unique goals, objectives, and tolerance for risk.

Bank products are FDIC-insured up to applicable limits, whereas insurance products are guaranteed by the financial strength and claims-paying ability of the issuing company.

Investments are subject to risk, including possible loss of principal.

KNOW THY RISK NUMBER

Knowing your unique tolerance for risk—and aligning your portfolio with it—provides the clarity you should have about your investments' potential risks. I tell my clients you can learn your risk tolerance in one of two ways: experience a market crash or know your risk number. If you know your risk number, and your financial house is designed in line with it, you are likely better poised to enjoy your retirement. Then when you turn on the news and see the S&P 500 tumbled 5 percent in a single day, you aren't worried about a financial storm because you know all of your money isn't in the roof.

After you know your financial house is strong enough to withstand a storm, the work doesn't end. The exterior of your financial house—investment planning—isn't just an empty shell. As we approach and enter retirement, we must do more than just worry about investment planning. If your house's exterior is investment planning, the interior consists of four distinct areas or rooms: income, healthcare, taxes, and legacy. To put it simply, your house's exterior is important because it influences the other rooms, which we will now explore.

We believe that proper risk allocation is arguably the most important step in having a strong financial house. If you would like to learn your unique risk number, visit our website and use our free tool: www.jbiance.com/risknumber.

What part of your current investment plan would you like to improve?

_____

_____

_____

_____

_____

_____

_____

_____

_____

_____

_____

_____

_____

_____

_____

_____

_____

CHAPTER 2

INCOME PLANNING
YOUR MASTER BEDROOM

A few months ago, my Aunt Sharon and Uncle Paul came to visit. Sharon and Paul are like grandparents to our kids and deeply loved for many reasons. One of the most exciting things about their visits is Aunt Sharon brings craft projects! One of the crafts Sharon brought for her recent visit was a foam sailboat project. After each of the kids built their sailboat, we headed to the creek. The baby couldn't participate, but the other six kids stood in a line across the creek and waited for the signal to start. The adults stood on the bridge that stretched over the creek about thirty yards downstream. I yelled, "Go!" and they all released their sailboats. At first, they were all sailing smoothly, but then river rocks, sticks, and small waves began taking them down one at a time. In the end, Mabel, the youngest of the competitors, made it to the finish line. There was laughing and cheering as Mabel's sailboat passed under the bridge.

Each of the kids built the same boat. They weren't specifically designed to take on the challenges that would come. Only one of the six made it to the end, and it was pure luck. Mabel got a different roll of the dice and came out the winner. I relate her victory correlates to what I often tell people: When you are young, you can leave things to chance; however, you need a plan when you approach retirement. An income plan helps get you to the finish line. In my experience, many Americans drift into retirement without a stress-tested income plan to make sure those dollars last. While you are working and saving for retirement, you can be largely unconcerned with positioning your money in retirement, and rightfully so. When you are working, you have time on your side. You can work—and play—without worrying too much about your future retirement income. As you move closer to retirement, things need to change.

There are two phases in an investor's life cycle: the accumulation phase and the distribution phase. If you are reading this book, you are probably approaching the distribution phase or have already entered it. These two phases could not be more different. When you approach retirement, you need a holistic plan. Yes, you need investment vehicles for your assets, but you really need a plan for distributing the assets you have worked a lifetime to accumulate. If you work with a retirement planner, or "retirement engineer" as I call it, the first interior room he will want to visit is the master bedroom, or income planning. If you don't have an income plan in retirement, you may have trouble sleeping at night.

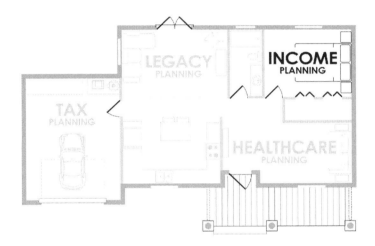

RISK AND YOUR INCOME

You cannot have a strong financial house unless it supports your income plan, which is a detailed projection of all of your retirement income streams. This plan should include stress-testing for market fluctuations, healthcare events, taxes, spousal/survivor benefits, and inflation. Your retirement income plan is the "punch list" for your master bedroom. In construction terms, a punch list refers to the work needed to be completed. After you have simulated the above scenarios, both independently and simultaneously, and have adjusted your plan to seek a high success probability, then you have an orderly room.

If you have worked with a financial advisor during the accumulation phase, there is a chance your financial house might be all roof investments and not designed for income. The specific focus of an "accumulation advisor" or a self-manager is *average rate of return*. Most investors have heard the importance of average rate of return, and therefore it alone becomes the goal in many cases. When you get close to retirement, however, the focus should shift from average rate of return to risk-adjusted return. Risk-adjusted return is often measured by a factor called the Sharpe ratio[3], which measures the efficiency of a portfolio.

To put it in layman's terms, it measures how much return we can potentially realize from the least amount of risk possible. That's what every retiree wants—low risk, high return. This equation is even more important in retirement because significant losses might not be made up later and can have a dire effect on income.

---

[3]Marshall Hargrave. Investopedia. April 25, 2020. "Sharpe Ratio" https://www.investopedia.com/terms/s/sharperatio.asp

Risk-adjusted return should be the priority for pre-retirees and retirees because, as we age, we run out of something: time! Once you have reached the distribution phase, you might not have the time to recover from a market correction. Time, however, is not the only factor. When you reach the distribution phase, you become much more vulnerable to the combination of other risks in relation to income, healthcare, taxes, and legacy. The truth is losses affect your portfolio more than gains no matter the season of your life. But combined with, for example, an income withdrawal or healthcare event, they can be dramatic. Let's look at an example on the next page.

ACCUMULATION PHASE

SUSAN			BETH		
Beginning Balance: $100,000 Yearly Withdrawal: $0.00			Beginning Balance: $100,000 Yearly Withdrawal: $0.00		
AGE	ANNUAL RETURN	*YEAR-END VALUE	AGE	ANNUAL RETURN	*YEAR-END VALUE
40	-14.31%	$85,690.00	40	27.49%	$127,490.00
41	-22.83%	$66,126.97	41	15.60%	$147,378.44
42	-16.00%	$55,546.66	42	22.50%	$180,538.59
43	22.24%	$67,900.23	43	-5.90%	$169,886.81
44	9.80%	$74,554.46	44	14.50%	$194,520.40
45	4.32%	$77,775.21	45	8.28%	$210,626.69
46	10.90%	$86,252.71	46	27.10%	$267,706.52
47	2.70%	$88,581.53	47	-2.20%	$261,816.98
48	-3.21	$85,738.06	48	14.70%	$300,304.07
49	21.00%	$103,743.06	49	19.00%	$357,361.85
50	16.70%	$121,068.15	50	32.90%	$474,933.90
51	5.30%	$127,484.76	51	11.10%	$527,651.56
52	-9.80%	$114,991.25	52	-9.80%	$475,941.71
53	11.10%	$127,755.28	53	5.30%	$501,166.62
54	32.90%	$169,786.77	54	16.70%	$584,861.44
55	19.00%	$202,046.25	55	21.00%	$707,682.34
56	14.70%	$231,747.05	56	-3.21%	$684,965.74
57	-2.20%	$226,648.62	57	2.70%	$703,459.82
58	27.10%	$288,070.30	58	10.90%	$780,136.94
59	8.28%	$311,922.62	59	4.32%	$813,838.85
60	14.50%	$357,151.40	60	9.80%	$893,595.06
61	-5.90	$336,079.47	61	22.24%	$1,092,330.60
62	22.50%	$411,697.35	62	-16.00%	$917,557.70
63	15.60%	$475,922.14	63	-22.83%	$708,079.28
64	27.49%	$606,753.14	64	-14.31%	$606,753.14
AVERAGE RETURN: 8.4%			AVERAGE RETURN: 8.4%		

Hypothetical example shown for illustrative purposes only and does not reflect the deduction of taxes or investment fees.

Susan and Beth are both forty years old, both in the accumulation phase, and they each have $100,000 invested. Neither Susan nor Beth are taking withdrawals from their portfolio (shown in the center column), and after a twenty-five-year period, they both end up at the same place. The only difference between Susan and Beth's experience in the market is the *sequence of returns*. A sequence of returns is the order in which an investor experiences returns. If you look closely, Beth's annual returns are identical to Susan's; she just experienced them in reverse order. As you can see, Susan *started* with three down years while Beth *ended* with three down years. But did it matter? No. In the end, they wind up with the *same average rate of return* and the same amount of money. Does it matter if you were Susan or Beth? No. Over this twenty-five-year period, it doesn't matter which way the dice fell—what sequence of returns they experienced.

Now let's look at Susan and Beth's experience for the next twenty-five years, during the distribution phase from age sixty-five to age eighty-nine. (*next page*)

DISTRIBUTION PHASE

SUSAN			BETH		
Beginning Balance: $606,753 Yearly Withdrawal: $36,000			Beginning Balance: $606,753 Yearly Withdrawal: $36,000		
Age	Annual Return	*Year-End Value	Age	Annual Return	*Year-End Value
65	-14.31%	$483,926.65	65	27.49%	$737,549.40
66	-22.83%	$337,446.19	66	15.60%	$816,607.11
67	-16.00%	$247,454.80	67	22.50%	$964,343.70
68	22.24%	$266,488.75	68	-5.90%	$871,447.43
69	9.80%	$256,604.65	69	14.50%	$961,807.30
70	4.32%	$231,689.97	70	8.28%	$1,005,444.95
71	10.90%	$220,944.17	71	27.10%	$1,241,920.53
72	2.70%	$190,909.67	72	-2.20%	$1,178,598.28
73	-3.21	$148,781.47	73	14.70%	$1,315,852.22
74	21.00%	$144,025.57	74	19.00%	$1,529,864.15
75	16.70%	$132,077.85	75	32.90%	$1,997,189.45
76	5.30%	$103,077.97	76	11.10%	$2,182,877.48
77	-9.80%	$56,976.33	77	-9.80%	$1,932,955.49
78	11.10%	$27,300.70	78	5.30%	$1,999,402.14
79	32.90%	$282.63	79	16.70%	$2,297,302.28
80	19.00%	($35,663.67)	80	21.00%	$2,743,735.76
81	14.70%	($76,906.22)	81	-3.21%	$2,619,661.84
82	-2.20%	($111,214.29)	82	2.70%	$2,654,392.71
83	27.10%	($177,353.36)	83	10.90%	$2,907,721.52
84	8.28%	($228,038.22)	84	4.32%	$2,997,335.09
85	14.50%	($297,103.76)	85	9.80%	$3,225,073.93
86	-5.90	($315,574.64)	86	22.24%	$3,943,002.37
87	22.50%	($422,578.93)	87	-16.00%	$3,276,121.99
88	15.60%	($524,501.24)	88	-22.83%	$2,492,183.34
89	27.49%	($704,686.64)	89	-14.31%	$2,099,551.90
AVERAGE RETURN: 8.4%			AVERAGE RETURN: 8.4%		

Hypothetical example shown for illustrative purposes only and does not reflect the deduction of taxes or investment fees.

What has changed? What has stayed the same? First, the returns are the same; just like the last graph, Susan experiences the same set of returns and Beth experiences them in reverse order. As a result, they both end up with the same average rate of return once again. While the sequence of returns and average rate of return have stayed the same, Susan and Beth are now in the distribution phase—they are both withdrawing $36,000 a year from their respective portfolios for their income (*see the center column in the graph above). Notice the main difference from the first graph: Susan runs out of money. You may be wondering," what happened?" Risk combined with withdrawals has drastically affected the outcomes for these two retirees.

Like Mabel's craft boat, Beth got lucky. Her first three years of drawing income were positive, so she experienced the good years first. On the other hand, Susan experienced three down years first and ultimately that is why her income plan failed. As you can see, at age eighty-nine, Beth has $2,099,551 but Susan runs out of money at age seventy-nine. The difference between their situations is sobering. Susan's withdrawals for income compounded the negative effect of her losses. How do you fix this problem? Building a strong financial house that doesn't leave things to chance puts you in a much better position for making sure you don't outlive your income.

As you can see from the previous graph, having a plan for your income is essential to not outliving your money. In 2019, financial planners reported their clients' top fear was running out of money in retirement, more than death.[4] Whether you fear outliving your money more than death or not, it is fair to say that income planning is important in retirement.

STRESS-TESTING YOUR INCOME PLAN

Ensuring your financial house is properly constructed for your season in life—the distribution phase—is only the beginning. There are unknowns in retirement that can have a significant impact on your income. If you do not have a roof, walls, and foundation, these unknowns can put you in a tight spot. For example, what if you have a healthcare event and need to withdraw a large sum of money, but the stock market is down 10 percent or 20 percent? You don't want to sell your positions because you would lock in a loss. First, proper planning would include an emergency fund, however, sometimes we need additional funds. If you don't have a foundation—a place from which to withdraw money without locking in losses—you have no choice but to take a hit. If you have a roof, walls, *and* a foundation, you can potentially draw income from your foundation without locking in losses and allow your roof and walls the opportunity to recover.

When it comes to designing your master bedroom, attention to detail is important. If you are working with

---

[4]Samiha Khanna, "Clients' Top Retirement Fear: Running Out of Money," Journal of Accountancy. (February 14, 2019). https://www.journalofaccountancy.com/news/2019/feb/top-retirement-fears-201920387.html

an advisor more suited for the accumulation phase, some key details in your income plan might be overlooked. In our practice, after we build an income plan, we stress-test it by running 1,000 Monte Carlo[5] simulations to model the probability of different outcomes. By doing this, we can give you a success probability estimate ranging from 0 percent to 100 percent.

Imagine getting on a plane, and after sitting down in your seat, the captain announces over the intercom, "Thanks for joining us for the flight today. We have clear skies, but only about a 55 percent chance of landing this plane safely." Would you stay on that plane? If you responded "Yes", I would venture to guess you enjoy gambling at the casino. In retirement, you want an income plan with a high success probability. Often, when a prospective client comes into our office and we stress-test their current method of withdrawing income, we find they have a low success probability. If you are worried that your plane (or your sailboat) might not make it to the finish line, it's time to renovate your master bedroom.

[5]Robert Stammers. Investopedia. Aug. 6, 2020. "Using Monte Carlo Analysis To Estimate Risk" https://www.investopedia.com/articles/financial-theory/08/monte-carlo-multivariate-model.asp

What part of your current income plan would you like to improve?

_____

_____

_____

_____

_____

_____

_____

_____

_____

_____

_____

_____

_____

_____

_____

CHAPTER 3

TAX PLANNING
STRATEGIES
YOUR GARAGE

Halloween is an exciting event in our home. My wife typically makes costumes for our kids, and we go door to door with several of our friends. When we return from trick-or-treating, one part of the evening is not particularly enjoyable for my kids, but I think it is a great time to teach a lesson. As they sit at the dining room table, dumping out their bags of candy, and counting their bounty, I make the feared announcement: "It's time to pay taxes!" Heads drop, and I make the rounds collecting my favorite chocolates (usually Kit Kats and Reese's Pieces). Learning about taxes isn't fun (especially for my kids), but it's a necessary room of your financial house.

As we continue to walk through your financial house, we come to the garage. I'm not sure about your garage, but mine has a lot more than a car in it. A garage is designed for cars, but somehow it gets cluttered. As you prepare for retirement, it's time to clean out the garage, and the best kind of garage is a clean one that simply holds your car. There are numerous analogies that I could use to describe the burden of taxes in retirement, such as a cluttered garage, but perhaps the best is debt.

If you have ever taken out a mortgage, it was most likely a fixed- rate mortgage. Most Americans choose a fixed-rate mortgage because they don't want the interest rate to change. If you have a tax-deferred account (IRA, 401(k), 403(b), SEP, etc.), unfortunately, you have an account that has one of the same features as a variable-rate mortgage. At any point, the IRS can change the rate (here, though, it is the tax rate rather than the interest rate). Like most garages, your tax-deferred account has more in it than just your money. Debt owed to the IRS clutters those accounts.

When you withdraw money from one of your tax-deferred retirement accounts, you must pay taxes on that money. Remember, withdrawing money from a tax-deferred retirement account is not an "if" but a "when" due to the fact that the IRS will eventually require you to withdraw money. Do you know what your tax rate will be one, five, or ten years from now? Is that within your control? Perhaps you want to withdraw as little as possible and leave it to your children. Do you know what taxes they will have to pay on those funds ten, twenty, or thirty years from now?

It doesn't take a financial analyst or CPA to look at our country's balance sheet and get the impression that we are heading in the wrong direction. The current United States debt exceeds $26 trillion.[6] Even some former government officials think the country may have to double the tax rates to solve our debt problem.[7] The

---

[6]As of July 2020. See https://treasurydirect.gov/govt/reports/pd/pd_debt-tothepenny.htm (for up to date figures)

[7]David McKnight, The Power of Zero, (Boston: Acanthus Publishing, 2013).

good news is that you can take steps to preserve some of your money in tax-free environments, thereby reducing your debt to the IRS. Before we review your options, however, let's first review the three types of tax buckets into which your money falls.

THE THREE TAX BUCKETS

The first tax bucket is the tax-deferred bucket. These are assets such as IRAs, 401(k)s, deferred annuities within a qualified retirement plan, etc. These accounts generally grow tax-deferred, which means you only pay taxes when you withdraw the money. You can buy and sell holdings inside your tax-deferred bucket, and you don't pay taxes on the gains until you withdraw the money. You may withdraw that money penalty-free after age fifty-nine and one-half and if you still have a balance at age seventy-two, the IRS will require you to take a minimum distribution (i.e. required minimum distributions or RMDs). If you neglect to withdraw the required amount, the current penalty is 50 percent of the RMD. Therefore, if you were required to withdraw $10,000 from your IRA and you did not, the penalty is $5,000! Not only that, you must still take the required distribution. This bucket may have benefited you while working—reducing your taxable income—but it can clutter your garage and create tax challenges in retirement.

The second bucket is the taxable bucket. This is the money you have probably already paid taxes on, and if you invest it, you pay taxes when you realize a return.

These are non-IRA assets such as brokerage accounts, savings accounts, or certificates of deposits at your bank. If you realize a gain in this bucket, you must pay the piper come April 15th of the following year.

The third bucket is the tax-free bucket. This money grows tax- free, and whether you withdraw your gains or leave it to your beneficiaries after your death, it is tax-free, subject to certain limitations. These assets include Roth IRAs and life insurance. I don't include municipal bonds in this bucket for a few reasons. The first is because to meet the requirement for the tax-free bucket, the asset must be free from federal tax, capital gains tax, and state tax. For example, suppose you live in North Carolina and purchase a municipal bond in Georgia. In that case, you aren't purchasing in the municipality you live in, so you would have to pay state taxes. Additionally, if you purchase a mutual fund of municipal bonds and your mutual fund increases and you decide to sell, you will likely pay capital gains tax.

❶	❷	❸
TAX-DEFERRED BUCKET	**TAXABLE BUCKET**	**TAX-FREE BUCKET**
IRAs, 401(k), Deferred Annuities	Brokerage, Savings, CDs	Roth IRAs, Life Insurance

Life insurance policy loans will reduce available cash values and death benefits and may cause the policy to lapse or affect any guarantees against lapse. Additional premium payments may be required to keep the policy in force. In the event of a lapse, outstanding policy loans in excess of unrecovered cost basis will be subject to ordinary income tax.

Roth IRA withdrawals are tax-free if taken after age fifty-nine-and-one-half, and the account has been open for at least five years. Annuity withdrawals are taxed as ordinary income, and if taken before age fifty-nine-and-one-half may incur an additional 10 percent federal penalty.

Bank products are FDIC-insured, whereas insurance and annuity guarantees are backed by the issuing company's financial strength and claims-paying ability.

As you review your portfolio, you will probably notice that you may have money in each of these three tax buckets. Now, let me ask you, in which bucket would you like to have most of your money? While you might prefer to have most of your money in the tax-free bucket, it is more common to have most of your money in the tax-deferred and taxable buckets. And again, the biggest concern is that the IRS can change the percentage that they can take from your money. Strategies for the tax-deferred bucket should address several factors, such as your age, income level, and estate value. To clean up your garage, however, you will have to be proactive. An accountant is concerned with the here and now while attempting to reduce the taxes you pay on last year's income. A holistic financial planner, however, is focused on the long term. If you are interested in being proactive, here are two strategies worth considering.

ROTH CONVERSIONS

In 1997, the Taxpayer Relief Act established the Roth IRA, named for its chief legislative sponsor, Senator William Roth of Delaware. Since then, the Roth IRA has been a popular account to grow money tax-free. Some conditions must be met to contribute to a Roth IRA, such as earned income, income level, and amount of contribution, so not everyone can contribute to a Roth IRA. However, converting your tax-deferred money to a Roth IRA is possible for everyone.

To illustrate the power of a Roth conversion, let's look at two hypothetical examples, one for a married couple and one for a single person.

Greg and Tina (Married Couple)
- Both age 65
- Goal is to convert $200,000 of an IRA (tax-deferred) to a Roth IRA (tax-free)

Darlene (Single)
- Age 65
- Goal is to convert $200,000 of an IRA (tax-deferred) to a Roth IRA (tax-free)

If Greg and Tina decide they want to convert $200,000 of their traditional IRA, and their other income streams total $75,000, their income for that year would be $275,000. It is important that they take into consideration the domino effect of substantially increasing income in any given year. It is possible to trigger more Medicare premiums, Social Security taxes, and capital gains taxes based on your income level. A Roth conversion must keep the big picture in mind, but if we look at the long-term savings of a Roth conversion, it can be significant.[8]

---

[8]Married Couple: Assumes living through age ninety, a 22.4% effective tax rate (combined federal and state) on RMDs and taxes paid on death, a 15% capital gains tax on reinvested RMDs, and a 5% average rate of return over the period. Single Person: Assumes living through age ninety, a 29.3% effective tax rate (combined federal and state) on RMDs and taxes paid on death, a 15% capital gains tax on reinvested RMDs, and a 5% average rate of return over the period. Example is for illustrative purposes only, is not guaranteed and should not be used as the basis for your own investment decisions.

GREG AND TINA

TRADITIONAL IRA		ROTH IRA	
Conversion Amount	$200,000	Conversion Amount	$200,000
Taxes on RMDs at age 72	$62,692	Taxes under current tax code	$46,000
Capital Gains Tax on reinvested RMDs	$26,796	Taxes on reinvested funds	$0
Taxes on value at death	$41,665	Taxes on value at death	$0
TOTAL TAXES PAID:	$131,153	**TOTAL TAXES PAID:**	$46,000

DARLENE

TRADITIONAL IRA		ROTH IRA	
Conversion Amount	$200,000	Conversion Amount	$200,000
Taxes on RMDs at age 72	$75,230	Taxes under current tax code	$60,000
Capital Gains Tax on reinvested RMDs	$29,610	Taxes on reinvested funds	$0
Taxes on value at death	$49,998	Taxes on value at death	$0
TOTAL TAXES PAID:	$154,838	**TOTAL TAXES PAID:**	$60,000

The examples above represent a 65 percent tax savings for Greg and Tina and a 61 percent tax savings for Darlene. Yes, you write one large check to the IRS during the year of the conversion, but then never have to send another if you follow the terms of the Roth IRA. As I mentioned previously, the long-term consequences of preserving your IRA can be significant.

I tell our teams of advisors all the time that one of the goals of our tax-planning strategies is to prevent our clients from having to pay taxes twice on the same money. If you convert a portion of your money to a Roth IRA, you can avoid this form of double taxation. However, converting to a Roth IRA isn't your only option. One other strategy is worth considering if you want to transition tax-deferred assets to a tax-free bucket, but you will need to play by a different set of rules.

SECTION 401(K)

Whether you know it or not, you are probably familiar with the United States Tax Code Title 26, Section 401(k). Sound familiar? It is the section of the tax codes that covers the creation, contribution, and withdrawal rules pertaining to tax-deferred 401(k) accounts. Most of the money saved by Americans for retirement is subject to this section of the tax law.[9] If you use a 401(k) as a savings vehicle, several stipulations will dictate the treatment of that account. Generally speaking, the IRS is happy to let you defer taxes while you are working and then require that you withdraw them later in life. Why? Well, let me ask you, if you could tax a farmer on his seed or his harvest, which would you prefer? The IRS allows you to defer paying taxes on the value of the seed only to step in and require taxes be paid on the typically much larger value of the harvest. Whether it is Section 401(k), Section 403(b), Section 457, or some other part of the tax code which governs tax-deferred

---

[9]Monique Morrissey, "The State of American Retirement Savings," Economic Policy Institute. (December 10, 2019) https://www.epi.org/publication/the-state-of-american-retirement-savings/

accounts, they all have the same end, taxes on the harvest.

If you are receiving a match in your 401(k), the compounding effect of those extra dollars can help cover the multitude of sins which I have just discussed. Yes, you are growing an account that will be taxed at harvest, but in most scenarios, the "free money" that your employer contributes keeps you ahead of the game. After you have contributed the necessary amount required for your match, you might want to consider an additional financial vehicle: life insurance.

SECTION 7702: "ROTH FOR THE WEALTHY"

In my experience, insurance is often poorly designed and over- sold, and some people have had a bad experience with it. If properly designed, however, life insurance can be an effective tool to not only provide a valuable death benefit for your loved ones but also provide an additional method of savings, potentially tax- free. How is this possible? Because with insurance, you get to play by a different set of rules.

Section 7702 of the United States Tax Code defines the tax treatment of life insurance. Under that section, if a life insurance contract is structured properly, gains can be withdrawn income tax-free.[10] Unlike a Roth IRA,

---

[10]Policy loans will reduce available cash values and death benefits and may cause the policy to lapse or affect any guarantees against lapse. Additional premium payments may be required to keep the policy in force. In the event of a lapse, outstanding policy loans in excess of unrecovered cost basis will be subject ordinary income tax.

there are no income limitations for contributing to life insurance. In his book *The Power of Zero*, David McKnight shares that more than 80 percent of Fortune 500 CEOs use life insurance as a tax shelter for their retirement savings as well as a legacy for their heirs.[11]

However, high-income earners are not the only group of investors who turn to life insurance. Pre-retirees and retirees are interested in this option because in addition to the death benefit and potential for tax-free income, if the contract includes the additional benefits of long-term care as discussed previously, they can kill two birds with one stone. And, of course, the death benefit is also tax-free. In summary, if you are looking for the following features, a permanent life insurance policy might be a consideration for you:

1. Tax-free death benefit for heirs
2. No income limitation on contributions
3. Tax-free growth
4. Tax-free withdrawals
5. Tax-free long-term care benefits (with the purchase of an added LTC rider)

Keep in mind, however, that because this is life insurance first and foremost, there are fees and charges, including surrender penalties for early withdrawals. You

---

[11]David McKnight, The Power of Zero, (Boston: Acanthus Publishing, 2013).

will need to qualify for the policy medically and perhaps financially and fund it appropriately for it to remain in force.

YOUR IRA IS AN IOU TO THE IRS

If you want the IRS to take the smallest bite possible out of your money, consider the strategies I've introduced that allow you to convert your tax-deferred money into tax-free money. Being proactive with cleaning out your garage is important for you and your heirs.

Sometimes I have clients tell me, "Justin, I am going to take my required minimum distributions, but I'm not worried about passing on my IRA. My kids can deal with the taxes." As I mentioned previously, many economists agree that tax rates will increase in the future, potentially leaving a much bigger burden than you realize. Additionally, with the 2019 passage of the Setting Every Community Up for Retirement Enhancement (SECURE) Act, with a few exceptions, your children can no longer stretch out distributions from an inherited IRA over their life-time. With this legislation, children now have to distribute those funds over ten years (unless certain conditions exist).[12]

The future tax burden your children might face is not the only reason you try to pay off that IOU to the IRS.

---

[12]H.R.1994 - Setting Every Community Up for Retirement Enhancement Act of 2019 https://www.congress.gov/bill/116th-congress/house-bill/1994/text

Let's say you are married, and you are trying to preserve your IRA for your spouse. Your spouse's income will be reduced after you pass away, and you don't want him/her to worry about outliving their income. While your intentions are pure, you forget that today you file your taxes at married filing jointly rates. After you pass away, your surviving spouse is subject to single filer rates, which are higher. If this happens, the surviving spouse could unintentionally write a much larger check to the IRS. Regardless of intention, if any room of your financial house is neglected, especially the garage, the clutter builds.

These strategies should be designed by professionals (both financial and tax) who specialize in this aspect of financial planning. You need advisors who can explain the benefits, limitations, and charges associated with any of the products recommended for your portfolio. You can implement other strategies to reduce the IOU you owe to the IRS, but regardless of the tool or design, the goal should always be to end up with a squeaky-clean garage.

What part of your current tax plan would you like to improve?

_____

_____

_____

_____

_____

_____

_____

_____

_____

_____

_____

_____

_____

_____

_____

_____

CHAPTER 4

HEALTHCARE PLANNING
YOUR LIVING ROOM

One Saturday afternoon when I was about twelve years old, my Mom and Grandpa were out running errands, and Grandma stayed home to watch us. I was outside playing most of the day, and when I came inside, Grandma wasn't in her recliner. I started walking around the house calling her name, but I wasn't getting a response. I checked her room and was startled to find her lying on the floor. My heart stopped. I shook her and she didn't respond. I felt helpless. I tried to sit her up against the wall and started yelling for someone to help. Thankfully, my

Mom was just returning home, and she quickly called 911. We learned later that Grandma had a stroke.

Most people I know can recall an experience or two in their lives when they felt helpless. With all of the quick fixes and conveniences of our modern-day culture, it is a feeling we don't encounter as often as past generations. As you approach retirement, however, there is a fair chance you might find yourself in a situation where you feel helpless and it will probably be related to healthcare. It is estimated that seven out of ten Americans will need some sort of long-term care in their lives.[13] With these kinds of odds, it is important that the living room of your financial house is in order. Knowing and communicating your desires to your loved ones and planning for the cost of long-term care, is an essential part of holistic financial planning.

---

[13]Glenn Ruffenach, "The Odds on Needing Long-Term Care," Wall Street Journal, (June 16, 2019). https://www.wsj.com/articles/the-odds-on-needing-long-term-care-11559836590

TRADITIONAL LONG-TERM CARE INSURANCE

Neither my grandma nor grandpa had a long-term care policy or other investment vehicle earmarked for long-term care expenses. My mom provided their long-term care as they got older, but most Americans aren't so fortunate. The national averages for the cost of care are significant.[14]

MONTHLY COST	2019
HOME HEALTH CARE	
Homemaker Services	**$4,290**
Homemaker Health Aide	**$4,385**
Based on annual rate divided by 12 months (assumes 44 hours per week).	
ADULT DAY HEALTH CARE	
Adult Day Health Care	**$1,625**
Based on annual rate divided by 12 months	
ASSISTED LIVING FACILITY	
Private, One Bedroom	**$4,051**
As reported, monthly rate, private, one bedroom	
NURSING HOME CARE	
Semi-Private Room	**$7,513**
Private Room	**$8,517**
Based on annual rate divided by 12 months	

In addition to the above costs for long-term care, the inflation rate of healthcare expenses is currently more than twice the standard inflation rates and things aren't

---

[14]Genworth. Cost of Care Survey 2019. https://www.genworth.com/aging-and-you/finances/cost-of-care.html

improving.[15] With the need for long-term care rising alongside the expense, it is important to know your options. Traditional long-term care insurance is not a solution we offer in our practice, and there are several reasons why it is not in our toolbox.

The primary reason we do not offer traditional long-term care insurance in our practice is that no life insurance company in the country will guarantee the premiums of the policy. If you purchase a long-term care policy, you might get a letter in the mail every other year or so that reads something like this: "Due to the rising cost of healthcare, the terms of your policy have changed. You may either elect to increase your premiums or reduce your benefits." The last thing you need during your retirement is to have a company change the game. I have heard this regret from retirees dozens of times, "I bought this policy and have budgeted to make sure I can cover the premiums, and now they are raising my premiums 25 percent!"

Another reason we don't offer traditional long-term care insurance is because it is a use it or lose it proposition. It is possible you could purchase a long-term care policy at age fifty-five, pay (potentially increasing) premiums on that policy for thirty years and then peacefully pass away in your sleep at age eighty-six. What does the

---

[15]Lucia Mutikani, "U.S. inflation firms on rising healthcare, energy costs," Reuters News Service, (November 13, 2019).https://www.reuters.com/article/us-usa-economy/us-inflation-firms-on-rising-healthcare-energy-costs-idUSKBN1XN1US

math look like on that? Well, if your policy started at $5,000 per year and the increases averaged 2.5 percent a year, you would have paid approximately $230,000 in premiums but never benefited from the policy coverage. It is kind of like automobile insurance, except it's significantly more expensive. The average auto insurance policy over that same period would have cost you approximately $32,000. If you never have an accident, it's unfortunate that you spent $32,000 in coverage over thirty years, but it is a lot less than $230,000. I know this all sounds like bad news, but some recent innovations in the insurance industry are now offering an alternative to traditional long-term care insurance.

LIFE INSURANCE FEATURES FOR CHRONIC ILLNESS

When most people hear the words, "life insurance," they typically cringe. They have flashbacks of an insurance agent coming to their homes and pushing a policy they are told they need but don't recall why. When a potential client walks into our office and shares their life insurance policies with us, we typically ask, "Why do you own this policy?" Most respond, "Because the life insurance agent said I needed it." Unfortunately, life insurance is "sold" more than it is "bought." When we provide life insurance to our clients it is typically for these three reasons: 1) their loved ones need income if they die, 2) they need long-term care, or 3) a large amount of their money is subject to taxes. I will cover how life insurance is used for tax purposes in the next chapter.

I am in the first group. I have seven children, and while my wife has multiple jobs—educating our children, caring for our household, running a small home business, and taking care of me (the most challenging)— she doesn't earn much income, although she is storing up treasures in heaven every day! If something were to happen to me, she would need an income to keep things going without me. This is the main purpose of term life insurance. If my wife is going to raise seven children for the next fifteen to twenty years, and then have an income for the remainder of her life, she needs a "self-completing" retirement plan. Using term life insurance, my retirement plan is completed immediately upon my untimely death, instead of when I am sixty-five. She'll need a large sum of money to replace income for a long time. Young families have a common need for this type of insurance. Term insurance is used less commonly by retirees. One appropriate use of term insurance for retirees would be to cover a debt obligation, with the term of the policy roughly matching the term of the debt obligation. If a spouse passes, the term policy's death benefit proceeds will pay off the debt, leaving the surviving spouse debt-free.

The second group I referenced above are those who need long- term care insurance. A select number of insurance companies allow the policyholder to access the death benefit for long-term care expenses. Yes, you read that correctly; you can use part of your death benefit while you are still living and need it most. These are often called either accelerated death benefit or chronic illness riders. If you cannot perform two of the six activities of daily living (i.e. transferring, toileting, bathing, getting dressed, eating, and continence), you can receive a portion of the death benefit of the policy to cover those costs. Life insurance policies with chronic illness riders either reimburse you *after* a qualifying expense has been paid (i.e., reimbursable method) or send you a portion of the death benefit *as soon as* qualifying conditions are met (i.e., indemnity method). There are benefits to each method. The reimbursable method provides some protection to the recipient of the coverage, as expenses must be claimed and approved by the insurance carrier. The indemnity method, on the other hand, has fewer restrictions on the use of funds. For example, if your house needs an entry ramp, the funds could be used for that construction project. If your policy rider requires you to access the benefit through the reimbursable method, you may not have this flexibility. But the indemnity method also introduces a risk. There have been cases where the funds received were not used by caregivers for the person who needs care. If the method is reimbursable, you don't have this risk.

THE "FREE" PART OF A LONG-TERM CARE PLAN

At this point, your head might be spinning. Between long-term care policies, chronic illness riders, indemnity method, reimbursable method, etc., you may be thinking this is too complicated. Why deal with it? Yes, long-term care strategies cost money and it is a room of your financial house that you don't want to renovate alone. The most important thing, however, isn't that you buy a product. The most important thing you can do when it comes to your future long-term care needs is that you have the necessary conversation with those who are closest to you.

When my dad's mother, Grandma Biance, got to the point that she needed long-term care, my dad and his two siblings met with her and came up with a plan. They decided to share the job of caring for her and divided the year into four months each. Grandma had a bedroom at each of their houses and it worked well for several years. She loved visiting with her three children and spending time with her nine grandchildren and twenty-one great-grandchildren as she transitioned from home to home. During the last few years of her life, she decided to remain with my dad full-time. He took care of her like a prince caring for his queen; it was beautiful to witness. Yes, there were costs involved, but Grandma lived to ninety-three, largely thanks to my dad and his siblings putting a long-term care plan together that did not include products. Difficult but worthwhile conversations and good relationships are often more powerful than financial resources.

CONVERSATIONS

Expenses related to long-term care can significantly impact the sustainability of your retirement plan. During the income planning phase of the Retirement Design System®, we always model a healthcare event to stress-test the plan and help ensure the plan we build for a client can endure. Just like your house, every room in your financial house is connected. For example, you could say the living room (healthcare plan) shares a wall with the master bedroom (income plan). If you have a healthcare event, it will likely impact your income. When it comes to purchasing life insurance, I encourage you to consult a dually licensed professional (licensed insurance agent + licensed investment advisor)to help you with your insurance needs. This is a room of your financial house you do not want to renovate alone.

I encourage you to have the necessary conversations with your loved ones about your desire for long-term care. Do you want to be in a nursing home, or do you want to age in place (home healthcare)? If you have children, do you want any of them to play a role? These conversations are difficult to initiate but I encourage you to sit down in your living room and talk about these things with your heirs. Start there and then work with a holistic planner who will help you establish a plan for the costs.

What part of your current healthcare plan would you like to improve?

_____

_____

_____

_____

_____

_____

_____

_____

_____

_____

_____

_____

_____

_____

CHAPTER 5

LEGACY PLANNING STRATEGIES
YOUR FAMILY ROOM

When I first started in financial services, one of my mentors strongly encouraged me to learn as much as possible about estate planning. He would always say, "Anyone who owns something and loves someone needs an estate plan." If you think about that saying, the logical conclusion is that everyone needs an estate plan. Estate planning is the "family room" of your financial house because if this room isn't orderly, your family—the people you love most—are at risk.

If you have ever been involved in settling an estate, you know that, unfortunately, the passing of the matriarch or patriarch of a family can often cause discord among the surviving family members. My book, *The Great Inheritance: 7 Steps to Leaving Behind More Than Your Money*, provides a framework for ensuring that your wealth transfer plan goes smoothly. In a sense, it is an entire book devoted to the family room of your financial house. And while I won't cover everything that is addressed in that book here, there are a few critical estate planning concepts worth noting.

When it comes to renovating your family room, two main areas need your attention: the financial and the non-financial. When financial advisors and attorneys discuss estate planning, the most common focus is on the legal and financial documents that need to be in place. While those aspects of legacy planning are important, research has shown that legacy planning should not overlook relational aspects.[16] You need to visit both the financial and the non-financial, the human and technical aspects of your family room. Therefore, before we cover the financial aspects, let's first look at two non-financial activities that can greatly improve your chance of a successful wealth transfer and an orderly family room. These activities: 1) capture your story, and 2) restore relationships within your family.

CAPTURE YOUR FAMILY STORY

Studies have shown that if your heirs know your story, both identity development and emotional well-being increase.[17] The first non-financial action to renovate your family room is to spend time capturing your family story. To put it simply, if you capture your family story, your heirs will have a stronger connection to you and the larger narrative that they are a part of, and not just the facts and figures of the estate.

When you think about your life events, it is helpful to think of both *historical* (H) and *formative* (F) experiences. Some family details are simply interesting to know and pass on to your children, while others are formative. Formative stories communicate the wisdom

[16]Roy Williams and Vic Preisser, Preparing Heirs, (San Francisco: Robert Reed Publishers, 2010).

[17]D. P. McAdams, "The psychology of life stories," Review of General Psychology 5, no. 2 (2001): 100-122.

you have acquired through your lifetime. And whether your children are your beneficiaries, or you are leaving your estate to charity or other family members, it is important they understand the journey that made you who you are.

To help get you started, below are a few questions you can use to reflect upon and record your historical and formative stories:

- What family traditions did you inherit from your parents/grandparents that you would like to see continued? (H)

- Was there a hardship that your ancestors endured that you have learned from? (H)

- Name something about rearing children (if you have them) that changed from your first child to your last. (F)

- What are you most proud of in your life? (H)

- How has your faith or spirituality changed throughout your life? Where did you start, and where are you now? (F)

- Was there any experience or event in your life that you didn't think you would overcome? How did you persevere, and what did that experience teach you? (F)

Let me give you an example of a formative story. Last year I was teaching a class at the local community college. The class is based on my book, *The Great Inheritance*. I explained the value of storytelling and how the principles we hold dear are often rooted in a story—an experience in life that was formative. John, one of the retirees in the class, said that he lives by the rule, "Never take shortcuts." I asked him to reflect on what life experience had formed that rule. John shared a story from middle school when he had taken a shortcut on a shop class project. His dad found out, drove him back to the school after hours, and insisted that he finish the project correctly. This was a deeply formative experience, and John was pleasantly surprised that one of his core values was rooted in a family story.

Sharing the stories that underpin the principles you hope to pass on is an effective way to communicate with your children and grandchildren. It is easy to say, "Son, never take shortcuts," but it is more difficult, and takes more humility to say, "Son, let me tell you about when I tried to take a shortcut and paid for it later." Taking time to record these stories and share them with your children—or family and friends if you don't have kids—will help strengthen your relationship with heirs.

RESTORE AND STRENGTHEN FAMILY BONDS

We have a few unique and non-negotiable rules that our kids learn from a very young age in our home. One of those rules is that the words "I'm sorry" and "It's okay" aren't allowed. If I have hurt someone, it is not *okay*, but it can be *forgiven*. If an apology is necessary, the words that we use are "Please forgive me" and "I forgive you." It is easy to blow through an attempt to apologize with the phrase, "I'm sorry," but it is more difficult to do that with, "Please forgive me." Likewise, it is easy to say, "It's okay," and not truly forgive. If you have children and you want your estate to transition smoothly, the first step in having an orderly family room" is to address what could be one of the most challenging areas of your life: reconciliation with your children.

I could share countless heartbreaking stories that I have heard from clients sitting in our conference room. Family life is hard, and it is challenging to go through life without experiencing conflict. My children are still young, and I cannot imagine how difficult it would be to have a long-standing rupture in my relationship with one of them. In my book, *The Great Inheritance*, I lay out a framework for reconciling and mentoring heirs. Since writing that book, I have received numerous letters from retirees sharing how they are on the path of reconciliation with their loved ones. I consider this one of the greatest fruits of writing that book.

After I proposed to Angela in that cold chapel, I asked a close friend, Dr. Bob Schuchts, if he would lead our marriage preparation. One of the principles I learned from Dr. Bob was a healthy understanding of a leader's role in a relationship. He challenged me as a future leader of our marriage. While this lesson was intended for a spousal relationship, I believe the principle works in many other relationships (e.g., father/son, mother/

daughter, manager/assistant, coach/player).

I remember sitting in Dr. Bob's office when this topic came up. He told me, "Justin, you and Angela will serve one another in your marriage, and you are equals, but there is one other area I would like you to take the lead on in your marriage, and it is a role that most men don't do very well." When he said this, I was a little nervous about what he would say next. He continued, "As a leader of your marriage, I want you to always initiate reconciliation."

This was unexpected and a bit confusing. My belief about reconciliation was that the person who had more fault in a conflict should be the one to initiate reconciliation. Then again, experience had taught me that method only led to either party initiating or one of the parties trying to reconcile but also accuse at the same time ("I'm sorry—but you know you had some fault here too.").

Dr. Bob continued, "Whether you feel your fault in a conflict is one percent or ninety-nine percent, I want you to initiate 100 percent of the time. I want you to be the first one to find your fault (the plank in your eye, not the splinter) and ask Angela for forgiveness, without expectation of reciprocation."

Wow, I thought, that is a tall order. When Dr. Bob said to initiate reconciliation, I had a feeling he didn't mean that after an argument I should go to Angela and say,

"Okay, this is how you hurt me, and I am ready for your apology." And when he handed me a Bible opened to Matthew 7:3—"Why do you observe the splinter in your brother's eye and never notice the great log in your own?"—it became clear what he meant. Trusting Dr. Bob, I wanted to implement his challenging words for two reasons: 1) I wanted to have a strong marriage, and 2) Most of the conflicts are my fault anyway.

As the matriarch and patriarch of your family, you are the leaders. Until you pass the torch of your family leadership to your heirs, you are the leader. And with this responsibility comes initiating reconciliation. Whether you have experienced small conflicts or large ones, initiating reconciliation is your job. Few things are more powerful than someone approaching you and asking forgiveness with no expectation of reciprocation.

Imagine that your father or mother is still alive. Imagine one of them coming to your home with an apology, a request for forgiveness with no focus on their own hurt. I remember where I was sitting when my dad called me and initiated reconciliation for the first time in our relationship. I was sitting on the front porch steps of my apartment in college. Was that a powerful experience? I remember which step I was sitting on. Few experiences are more powerful than when a parent asks a child for forgiveness.

In terms of the non-financial aspects of estate planning, I encourage you to engage with your children. If you find the plank and initiate reconciliation without expectation of reciprocation, the rest will be easy. I have witnessed people talking in circles for hours trying to resolve a conflict because they don't start there.

Your relationship with your children might be strong, it might be cordial, or it might be on the rocks. Regardless of where on the spectrum your relationship with your children falls, there is always room for improvement. If you devote time and energy to restoring and strengthening the relationships in your family, you will visit an area of your family room few have the courage to visit.

BASICS OF ESTATE PLANNING

While it is important not to skip over the non-financial aspects of designing your family room (capturing your family story and restoring relationships), the room isn't complete without getting financial and legal documents in order. As we review the legal aspects of your family room, I will refer to four primary documents:

> Durable General Power of Attorney
>
> Living Will/Healthcare Surrogate
>
> Last Will & Testament
>
> Revocable Living Trust (if needed)

When prepared properly with the assistance of an estate planning attorney, these documents can help ensure your wealth transfers to your heirs or loved ones in accordance with *your* desires – and *as you willed*. According to a survey conducted by US Legal Wills, 63 percent of respondents had no will at all, and only half of those over age sixty-five had a will that was up to date.[18] If you die without a will, you cede control of your assets to the state in which you lived. The state's laws will determine who your heirs will be, and the state will also choose the executor of your estate. Think about that for a moment. Do you want the state deciding who your heirs are and who will manage your affairs after your death? Most would say that this is the one entity they absolutely do not want meddling in their business and making decisions on their behalf. Why then do so many people die without a will? A recent survey of 2,000 Americans found that two of the main reasons so many people die without a will are procrastination and cost.[19] In our practice, I find that cost is sometimes a concern, but for most retirees, it comes down to plain old procrastination.

Don't procrastinate! It could burden your family with both financial and non-financial struggles that make a difficult time worse if you do. In their book *5 @ 55*, attorneys Judith Grimaldi and Joanne Seminara suggest that all people complete their estate documents by—

---

[18]Tim Hewson, "Are there even fewer Americans without wills?" U.S. Legal Wills, Accessed Aug. 9, 2017. https://www.uslegalwills.com/blog/americans-without-wills/

[19]"Make-a-Will Survey," Rocketlawer.com.

yes, you guessed it—age fifty-five.[20] Whether you are forty-five, fifty-five, sixty-five, or seventy-five—if you own something and you love someone, you need an estate plan. If you would like a free tool to help you get started, simply email learn@jbiance.com and ask for our Estate Planning Workbook. While we don't offer estate planning services ourselves, we do often team up with our client's legal representatives to ensure their estate plan aligns with a holistic financial plan.

LOAD-BEARING

We conclude the legacy planning phase of our process by providing what we call a legacy retreat to our clients. We sit down with our clients and their heirs and slowly walk through the legal documents together. We don't discuss *dollars and cents*; we simply discuss *roles and responsibilities*. This gives the heirs of our clients a chance to ask questions for clarification and provides an opportunity for our clients to elaborate on their desires if they so choose. I always share with the heirs that the next time we sit down together will probably be when one of your parents has died. But instead of division and discord, we should have clarity and good communication. Most Americans simply mail a copy of their legal documents to their children. If you want your passing to bring your family closer together rather than push them apart, a meeting with your heirs can help. After the financial part of the retreat, we move

---

[20]Judith D. Grimaldi and Joanne Seminara, 5@55 (Fresno: Quill Driver Books, 2015).

on to the non-financial part and together draft a family charter. This special project leaves the heirs with a memorialized statement of the family's values, a vision that can be passed on for generations to come.[21]

As you can see, it will take time and attention to make sure the financial and non-financial aspects of your family room are in order. **This is a chapter that might be worth re-reading at some point**. When it comes to your financial house, every wall of the family room is load bearing. If this room is not strong and orderly, it could impact every other room in the house. When I encourage my clients to start working on this room, I recommend taking baby steps—for both the non-financial and the financial. Perhaps a good start is scheduling a complimentary consultation with your attorney or writing a short letter to an estranged child (only addressing the plank), but regardless of the step you take, take one. An orderly family room will strengthen your financial house.

---

[21]The Great Inheritance: 7 Steps for Leaving Behind More Than Your Money, (Crescat Press, February 20, 2018).

What part of your current legacy plan would you like to improve?

_____

_____

_____

_____

_____

_____

_____

_____

_____

_____

_____

_____

_____

_____

_____

_____

CHAPTER 6

CHOOSING A RETIREMENT ENGINEER

W e don't have cable in our home, but if we did, I know which station would be most-watched: HGTV. Our love for renovating homes started during that first old apartment renovation and hasn't changed since. When Angela and I are on a trip and have access to cable, she gets caught up on the channel's various home renovation shows. If you asked my children what cable is, they would probably respond by telling you it is HGTV.

The show *Fixer Upper* gained incredible popularity. If you have never seen the show, co-hosts Chip and Joanna Gaines renovate houses in their hometown of Waco, Texas. What I find interesting about the show is the amount of planning and expertise that goes into every project. And not just the expertise and planning of Chip and Joanna, but also their partners, sub-contractors, and suppliers.

Let's say you were about to renovate your kitchen. Would you rather do it yourself or hire an expert? Let me ask that question a different way. If money weren't an issue and you could either do the work yourself or hire an expert like Chip and Joanna, which would you choose? With the former, everything falls on your shoulders, the decisions and the work. With the latter, you still get to make the decisions (pick out the cabinets, choose the paint color, etc.) but you have the best advisors in the business partnering with you to help you make those decisions. Some would choose to do all the work themselves, but I suspect the majority would hire Chip and Joanna if it were possible.

The planning and expertise required to renovate your financial house is significant. Financial renovation is perhaps one of the most important projects of your life, and the consequences of not leveraging the planning systems and product knowledge of professionals could be the difference between a solid versus flimsy construction. But with more than 600,000 people licensed as financial services advisors in the country, how do you find the right one?[22] If you want to renovate your financial house so that it's ready for retirement living, you need to make sure your financial advisor is genuinely qualified as someone able to design your house for the retirement season of life. I will propose three criteria that your advisor should meet: dually licensed, held to the fiduciary standard, and independent.

INSURANCE ONLY VERSUS DUALLY LICENSED

If you think that the financial services industry is too complicated and not transparent enough, I agree. One of the unique problems to financial services is that you sometimes have competition for business where there doesn't have to be competition. For example, if you are remodeling your home, the electrician and the plumber aren't going to compete to get hired. You need electricity and you need running water. You are not going to invest in one and not the other. In financial services, however, different financial professionals are often vying for the same business. Let's say you want to build a strong financial house. Based on your risk tolerance number, you want to put 40 percent of your money in the roof (e.g. equities), 20 percent of your money in the walls (e.g., corporate bonds), and 40 percent in the foundation (e.g., insurance products). If you sit down with a professional who is only securities licensed, do you think he will like that plan? Maybe not. He might want most of your money invested in securities. Or

[22]FINRA. Media Center: "Statistics." 2020. https://www.finra.org/media-center/statistics

perhaps you attend a dinner seminar and schedule a meeting with the presenter who is an insurance agent. Do you think he would encourage investing 60 percent of your money in the securities world? Likely not. He will probably want you to focus on only insurance products (annuities and life insurance). When looking for a holistic financial advisor, you want to find someone who is dually licensed, an advisor who has both a securities license (permitted to provide investment advice and products) and an insurance license (can recommend insurance products). Working with a financial professional who has access to both the securities world and the insurance world—as long as he/she is independent and is held to the fiduciary standard—will give you access to the largest selection of quality products for building your financial house.

BROKER VERSUS FIDUCIARY STANDARD

When an aspiring financial professional wants to get licensed, two different paths are available. He can choose a license that holds him to the *fiduciary standard*—recommendations in the client's best interest—or choose a license that holds him to a *suitability standard*—recommendations suitable for the client. A fiduciary is someone who, by law, *must put your interests above their own*. Attorneys have similar legal requirements as fiduciary advisors. An attorney who fails the attorney-client relationship through a breach of fiduciary duty could be disbarred. Something similar is true for a financial advisor.

Financial professionals who are subject to a fiduciary standard are called investment advisor representatives and work for a registered investment advisor. A financial professional who is only subject to a suitability standard is called a registered representative and works for a broker-dealer.

You may be wondering about the difference between these two standards. Could a recommendation be suitable and not be in your best interest? Yes. For example, as an investor, you may have enough liquidity in your portfolio to purchase a variable annuity (the purchase is suitable). Still, due to high fees and surrender charges, it might be better for the broker selling the variable annuity (commissions) than it is for you. Does this mean that all brokers are out to do what is in their best interest and not yours? No. A broker can do what is in your best interest, *but an advisor held to the fiduciary standard is required by law to do what is in your best interest.* It is important that you understand the specific licensing and certifications your financial professional has prior to hiring him as your financial advisor, sort of like your own retirement engineer.

CAPTIVE VERSUS INDEPENDENT

A friend of mine, who used to work for a large retail brokerage company, told me that every portfolio he built for a prospect was based on the company's three investment recommendations: 1) American Funds, 2) American Funds, and 3) American Funds. Perhaps you are familiar with this scripture: "No one can serve two masters; for either he will hate the one and love the other, or he will be devoted to the one and despise the other."[23] I have found that these words apply to several areas of my life, and one of those is my work with retirees. Financial professionals are either captive, which generally means they work for a publicly traded company (e.g., Edward Jones, Ameriprise, Merrill Lynch, Morgan Stanley, etc.), or they work for an independent firm. If I worked for a publicly traded company, I would essentially have two bosses: my private client and the public company. I might have quotas to make and proprietary products to sell in order to support a stock price, and at the end of the day, if I didn't produce, I could lose my job. But what if producing for a boss or shareholders conflicts with my client's interests? As an independent advisor, I do not have a boss on Wall Street dictating to me how many clients I should acquire or what products I should recommend.

Captive professionals who work for retail brokerage firms are sometimes under sales pressure. There are two main reasons for this. The first is because the company's stock is publicly traded and, therefore, not only do professionals have clients to serve, but their bosses also have shareholder expectations to manage. The second is because retail brokerage firms have contracts with mutual fund companies that provide revenue sharing. Revenue sharing is an agreement made between a broker and a mutual fund company. If the broker sells a

---

[23]Matthew 6:24 RSV

certain volume of the mutual fund company's products (mutual funds), the mutual fund company provides a kickback to the broker. For example, American Funds wrote a check to Edward Jones for $92.8 million in 2019![24] Yes, Edward Jones sold so many shares of American Funds products that they profited an extra $92 million for doing so. I suggest you don't settle for a captive professional. Choose an independent advisor who is accountable by law to put your interests first (fiduciary) and does not have a boss on Wall Street.

RETIREMENT ENGINEER

The day I cut our bedroom carpet too short in Grandmother Hartley's apartment ended up being a very frustrating day. My brother, Jason, was with me, and while we should have quit after our miscalculation, we continued installing the carpet. Yes, it was too short, but we decided we would just use a remnant to cover the hole and install it anyway. We moved the carpet stretcher into place—a tool neither of us had ever used—and then I began to push with all my might. It was at this moment that we learned a very important lesson. It is imperative that the end of the stretcher, which is pushing against the opposite wall, is placed at the base of the wall. We didn't know that, and as I pushed, the carpet stretcher went through the wall. I looked back and Jason was standing next to the wall with his jaw on the floor. As you can imagine, between cutting the carpet

---

[24]"2019 Revenue Sharing Disclosure," Edward Jones, December 31, 2016. https://www.edwardjones.com/images/revenue-sharing-disclosure.pdf.

too short and then putting the stretcher through the wall, I have had better days. Since Jason is the analyst in the family, I still blame him for not researching the details of how to use a carpet stretcher before we started the project.

Renovating a house can be challenging, especially if it isn't your day job. Prospective clients walk into our office every week feeling a bit overwhelmed about their current situation. Questions like, "Am I paying too much in fees?" or "Am I invested too risky for retirement?" or "Do I have bad products?" are swirling in their minds. They often have an intuitive sense that something needs to change, but they just can't put their finger on it. Had I known how difficult replacing that carpet would have been, I would have done things differently. I would have done more due diligence before starting, I would have taken my time, and I would have sought the help of a professional—not just any professional, but one who had a time-tested process to help me achieve my goals.

If you are working with a financial advisor, I believe they should be independent, dually licensed, and held to the fiduciary standard. They should have a time-tested and systematic process for building a custom retirement plan. As I am sure you have gathered while reading this book, the distribution phase of retirement takes more intentional planning, and frankly, more work. Our grandparents didn't have a retirement engineer taking care of every room of their financial house.

If reading about our process motivates you to bring these questions to your current advisor, I suggest you reconsider. If your current advisor hasn't already designed a plan for these five areas of retirement (investment, income, healthcare, taxes, and legacy), I believe that he or she is already a step behind you. Your advisor should be a step ahead of you. You shouldn't have to advise your advisor. It's time for a second opinion from a dually licensed, independent advisor who is held to the fiduciary standard and has a time-tested planning process. Don't trust your financial house with anyone else. There is no reason to settle.

As you read about the attributes of a holistic financial advisor, what thoughts came to mind?

_____

_____

_____

_____

_____

_____

_____

_____

_____

_____

_____

_____

_____

_____

_____

_____

CHAPTER 7

FOCUSING ON YOUR WHY

YOUR FRONT PORCH

After years of home renovations and moving around in Florida, Angela and I decided it was time to set roots. For several years we discerned where we felt called to raise our family and eventually decided it would be western North Carolina. Some longtime friends had introduced us to the area, and we decided to buy a house on seven acres in Tryon, North Carolina. Angela and I fell in love with the natural beauty of the property—hills to hike, a creek to play in, and mountain views. The house needed a lot of work, but well, we were used to that.

The biggest thing the house was missing was a front porch. The beautiful north-facing view could be enjoyed from many windows, but there wasn't that quintessential North Carolina front porch.

We were in the house for a few weeks when my handy Uncle Greg called and asked if he and my Aunt Kim could help with anything. I jokingly said, "Well, I would love to add a front porch to the house," to which he responded, "That sounds like fun. Let's do it!" The next month, Aunt Kim and Uncle Greg came to visit for a week. Before he arrived, I poured footers, purchased the lumber, and laid out the plan. We worked from sunup to sundown for a solid week and when they left, all that remained to do was lay the deck boards.

Our front porch has been a wonderful place of leisure. Sipping coffee on a Saturday morning, watching the sheep graze, or enjoying conversation with family and friends are all possible, in part thanks to that front porch. The front porch is also a way of gauging how busy we are. If life is getting too cluttered with running here and there and not resting and enjoying life, the front porch is our reminder. If it's been a while since we've sat on the front porch, we know it's time to slow down.

In a sense, retirement is like that front porch, only that you have worked thirty to forty years to build it, not a week. You have created a place to sit back, relax, and enjoy the more important things in life. Building the front porch was your career, your job. Now that it is built, making sure you are able to enjoy that porch is the job of a retirement engineer.

How does a financial advisor help you spend time on your front porch? By designing a strong financial house, so you don't have to worry unnecessarily about it. How can you gaze out from your front porch if you are worried about the strength of the structure behind you? With a strong financial house, it is time to turn your attention to living retirement richly, beginning with leisure.

LIVING RETIREMENT RICHLY

Being at leisure and finding fulfillment living a rich retirement can be challenging. What is leisure? Leisure is turning your gaze to reality. It is being receptive to the people and places of your life without the constant need to be "productive". It is difficult for almost everyone in today's culture, and retirement doesn't make leisure an instant habit. What retirement does do, however, is place leisure a bit more within your reach. In a way, you are now part of the leisure class. If you have a strong financial house, your income is reliable, so you can turn your attention to higher, leisurely activities. I find that most retirees are just as busy, if not busier, than they were when they were working. I often hear a retiree explain, "I don't know how I got anything done when I worked. I am retired now, and I can barely keep up!" This is good as long as the activity is both good for your body and your soul.

The transition from working to retirement is something that shouldn't be taken lightly. I have witnessed numerous retirees struggle with finding purpose in retirement. If you were productive for thirty, forty, or fifty years, it could be hard to kick back and enjoy your front porch. Being active in retirement isn't a bad thing. The idea is to spend your retirement years focused on opportunities you spent a lifetime working to create. Sometimes it is difficult to see the whole wheel turning when you are part of the machine. At this stage in life, you have a better vantage point than you had in the past. Again, keeping busy in retirement is extremely important. You may have heard the adage "when you retire you expire" so yes, activity and even work are good. What retirement gives you is the freedom to *keep working*, but rather than working for a wage, you get to work for what is important to you. But leisure is more than work. It is taking dance classes, writing your grandchildren, reading a good book, watching sheep graze. Yes, keep busy, but make leisure part of your daily retirement rhythm.

FOCUS ON YOUR WHY

As I shared at the beginning of this book, I grew up living with Grandma and Grandpa. Grandpa taught me how to drive a car, and Grandma taught me how to sit and enjoy the presence of another person. Whenever they were distracted or agitated by a challenging situation, it usually had to do with one of the five areas of our planning system, one of the five areas of their financial house: investment, income, healthcare, taxes, or legacy. Their experiences in retirement compelled my brother, Jason, and I to create The Retirement Design System®. The system devises planning strategies in the areas we saw lacking in our grandparents' lives. Living retirement richly has nothing to do with money. If you are living retirement richly, the concerns and challenges money can present simply vanish. Why do you want your concerns about money to vanish? Is it to lower your blood pressure, make life easier, or help you sleep better at night? While those might be worthy reasons, the primary reason to have a strong financial house is so you can focus on your goals—your why.

I don't know about you, but it's hard for me to sit down in a messy room and enjoy myself. In our home, we do "five-minute clean-ups." We set a timer, and the whole family picks up the room. Whether we are planning to pray, read, watch a movie, or play a board game together, everyone in our family enjoys a clean room. It's easier to focus on our goal if the room is clean. Ultimately, the purpose of this book is to help you focus on your goals, your why. Why did you retire? Why do you get out of bed this morning? Every retiree I know has a why (or a few whys). It is my job to make sure that their financial concerns do not cloud their focus. With a financial house renovated for retirement and designed to last, your days can be filled with focusing on your Why. My hopes and prayers are that, in some small way, this book has helped you do just that.

What is/will be most important to you in retirement? List the people and activities that you will focus on in retirement.

_____

_____

_____

_____

_____

_____

_____

_____

_____

_____

_____

_____

_____

_____

_____

_____

QUESTIONNAIRE

RETIREMENT RENOVATION QUESTIONNAIRE

Working with hundreds of pre-retirees and retirees over the years I have found that most of them do not receive the planning they deserve. The questions below are not an exhaustive list, but they will provide a little insight into what good planning looks like. If you are uncertain or answer no to any of them, I invite you to visit our website (www.jbiance.com) and schedule an appointment with one of our advisors. We would be honored to help you build a holistic plan designed to last.

INVESTMENT PLANNING

1. Do you know your risk tolerance (more specifically, your *risk number*) and the amount you could lose if you experienced a market correction or crash?

   ☐ Yes   ☐ No

2. Do you understand what type of investments you own?

   ☐ Yes   ☐ No

3. Do you know how much you are currently paying in fees and do you receive more than just investment planning for those fees?

   ☐ Yes   ☐ No

4. Does your financial house have a foundation or is it only made of roof and wall investments?

   ☐ Yes   ☐ No

5. Does your current portfolio have the protection, guarantees, and tax benefits of insurance-based assets?

   ☐ Yes   ☐ No

6. Are you able to identify low quality retail holdings in which you may be paying higher fees and load charges?

   ☐ Yes   ☐ No

INCOME PLANNING

1. Do you have a detailed distribution plan in place that projects all your streams of income from now until age 100?

   ☐ Yes ☐ No

2. Do you have a spousal continuation plan in place that details how a surviving spouse will make up lost income due to the first spouse passing?

   ☐ Yes ☐ No

3. If you have an income plan, has it been stress-tested for a healthcare event?

   ☐ Yes ☐ No

4. If you have an income plan, has it been stress-tested for a market correction or crash?

   ☐ Yes ☐ No

5. Do you have a plan for how your strategy changes if any of the events above take place?

   ☐ Yes ☐ No

6. Have you reviewed income planning strategies related to your Social Security income?

   ☐ Yes ☐ No

7. Are your assets producing enough of a reasonable return in order to maintain pace with inflation?

   ☐ Yes ☐ No

TAX PLANNING STRATEGIES

1. Have you classified your assets into the three tax buckets, where appropriate?

   ☐ Yes   ☐ No

2. Does your advisor meet with your CPA or accountant to help ensure your estate is structured as tax-efficiently as possible?

   ☐ Yes   ☐ No

3. Are your current life insurance policies reviewed annually to ensure proper cash value, a sustainable death benefit, and to assess other policy features?

   ☐ Yes   ☐ No

4. Are you currently implementing strategies to transition assets in the tax-deferred bucket into the tax-free bucket where appropriate?

   ☐ Yes   ☐ No

5. Do you have an appropriate amount of your tax-deferred assets in the foundation, so that you are not forced to lock in losses during a down market due to required minimum distributions (RMDs)?

   ☐ Yes   ☐ No

6. Are you currently repurposing your RMDs in order to increase your inheritable estate?

   ☐ Yes   ☐ No

HEALTHCARE PLANNING

1. Has your current advisor spoken with you about long-term care—not necessarily offered you a product to purchase, but asked you what your desires are for your care?

   ☐ Yes   ☐ No

2. Are your long-term care policies reviewed annually?

   ☐ Yes   ☐ No

3. Do you have a living will and/or healthcare surrogate?

   ☐ Yes   ☐ No

4. If you have a healthcare surrogate, is he or she local, and do they have a copy of your healthcare directive?

   ☐ Yes   ☐ No

5. If you are incapacitated, have you verbally shared (in addition to the documents) with your loved ones your desires for your healthcare?

   ☐ Yes   ☐ No

6. Has your advisor reviewed your Medicare supplemental insurance options with you, and are you currently receiving the best value for the monthly premium that you pay?

   ☐ Yes   ☐ No

7. Does your current life insurance include long-term care benefits in the event that you become terminally ill or cannot perform two of the six activities of daily living (transferring, toileting, bathing,

getting dressed, eating, and continence)?

☐ Yes   ☐ No

LEGACY PLANNING STRATEGIES

1. Do you have a Last Will & Testament or Revocable Living Trust that is current and consistent with your desires?

    ☐ Yes   ☐ No

2. Do you have current financial and healthcare powers of attorney?

    ☐ Yes   ☐ No

3. Do you have a summary of all of your assets with up to date primary and contingent beneficiaries in place?

    ☐ Yes   ☐ No

4. Has your advisor offered to meet with you, your attorney, and your heirs, to explain in detail how your estate is structured, and help prepare the person you have appointed to lead the wealth transfer process?

    ☐ Yes   ☐ No

5. Have you reviewed your legal documents for additions or changes in the last five years?

    ☐ Yes   ☐ No

6. Have you reviewed any personally owned investment properties for liability issues and vulnerabilities to lawsuits?

    ☐ Yes   ☐ No

7. If you own a business, do you have a business succession plan in place?

☐ Yes ☐ No

QUESTIONS FOR REFLECTION—CHOOSING A FINANCIAL ADVISOR

1. Can you walk into your home office and pull a holistic retirement plan from the shelf that includes an investment plan, income plan, healthcare plan, tax plan, and legacy plan?

☐ Yes ☐ No

2. Does your advisor meet with you at least biannually to review the above areas and adjust your plan according to your goals or changes in your life?

☐ Yes ☐ No

3. Does your advisor have the licenses and expertise to advise you on investments and products that span both the securities world and the insurance world?

☐ Yes ☐ No

4. Does your advisor have a defined and holistic planning process that involves more than simply investing your money?

☐ Yes ☐ No

5. Does your advisor work for an independent firm, one that operates outside of the influences of a publicly traded company, product quotas, or revenue-sharing agreements?

☐ Yes ☐ No

6. Does your advisor have a local office in the town in which you live?

   ☐ Yes   ☐ No

LIVING RETIREMENT RICHLY

1. If you are preparing for retirement, do you worry about your money often?

   ☐ Yes   ☐ No

2. If you are retired, are you enjoying the more important things in life, or have the worries and/or work of retirement started to feel like a part-time or full-time job?

   ☐ Yes   ☐ No

3. Is there a hobby or leisure activity that you have always wanted to adopt, but you haven't gotten around to it?

   ☐ Yes   ☐ No

4. Are your goals or bucket list items reviewed and discussed every time you meet with your financial advisor?

   ☐ Yes   ☐ No

5. Are you spending as much quality time with your friends and family that you had hoped you would spend in retirement?

   ☐ Yes   ☐ No

6. Are you able to focus on what matters in life without worrying about outliving your money?

   ☐ Yes   ☐ No

ABOUT THE AUTHOR

Justin M. Biance, CEP®
CHIEF EXECUTIVE OFFICER

Justin is a financial advisor, insurance professional, and Certified Estate Planner™. In addition to *Designed to Last*, Justin is the author of *The Great Inheritance: 7 Steps to Leaving Behind More Than Your Money*. He is co-founder of J. Biance Financial (www.jbiance.com) and the Retirement Design System®, which helps pre-retirees and retirees create confidence in every area of retirement. He is also the host of the radio show *Retirement Design with the Biance Brothers*, which airs in Florida and North Carolina.

Justin holds two graduate degrees, a Master of Science in entrepreneurship from the University of Florida and a Master of Arts in theology from Holy Apostles College and Seminary. He also founded Fraternus, Inc. — a faith-based mentoring organization for young men. Justin's greatest joy is spending time with his wife, Angela, and their seven children.

Made in the USA
Columbia, SC
13 February 2025

53700369R00065